Readers

PHOTOGRAPHS BY
HARVEY FINKLE

A BOOK OF POSTCARDS

POMEGRANATE ARTBOOKS

SAN FRANCISCO

Pomegranate Artbooks
Box 6099
Rohnert Park, CA 94927

Pomegranate Europe Ltd.
Fullbridge House, Fullbridge
Maldon, Essex CM9 4LE
England

ISBN 0-7649-0044-7
Pomegranate Catalog No. A876

Pomegranate publishes books of
postcards on a wide range of subjects.
Please write to the publisher for more information.

Designed by Young Jin Kim
Printed in Korea
05 04 03 02 01 00 99 98   10 9 8 7 6 5

To facilitate detachment of the postcards from this book, fold each card along its perforation line before tearing.

Reading is so commonplace an activity that recording its occurrence might seem pointless—but when caught by the intuitive eye of photographer Harvey Finkle, it is anything but. With his uncanny sense of timing and his intimate approach to traditional street photography, Finkle creates images that not only are pleasing to look at but also evoke an emotional response, highlighting both the humor and the underlying pathos in the solitary act of reading. Look at the photograph, for example, of the man sitting cross-legged on the floor of the Philadelphia Museum of Art, so caught up in his book that he is unaware of the painted gorilla apparently reading over his shoulder, or the photograph of the young woman reading on a subway platform, seemingly oblivious to the train whizzing past just inches from her face. Finkle's images of city dwellers engrossed in their reading are somehow comforting, offering testimony that our hectic, impersonal modern world is, after all, civilized enough to shelter a reader who momentarily loses track of time and place. Whether commuting to work, lingering over coffee, or passing the time on a park bench, each of the subjects pictured here occupies that private island of calm and quiet in which the rest of the world falls away in the magical merging of reader and written word. If you are a reader—if you, like those pictured here, believe the printed word to be both a source of pleasure and a passport to a vast world of knowledge and understanding—you will enjoy this simple yet eloquent homage to the act of reading.

Harvey Finkle's photographic projects range from a documentation of the resettlement of Indochinese refugees to an audiovisual slide show depicting the ravages of Alzheimer's disease on patients and families. His work has been displayed in more than two dozen venues, including Painted Bride, Harkness House, and the New York Public Library.

Readers

Photographs by Harvey Finkle
Philadelphia, 1980

POMEGRANATE BOX 6099 ROHNERT PARK CA 94927

Readers

Photographs by Harvey Finkle

Tucson, 1988

POMEGRANATE BOX 6099 ROHNERT PARK CA 94927

Readers

Photographs by Harvey Finkle
Lancaster, Pennsylvania, 1984

POMEGRANATE BOX 6099 ROHNERT PARK CA 94927

Readers

Photographs by Harvey Finkle
New York, 1982

POMEGRANATE   BOX 6099   ROHNERT PARK   CA   94927

Readers

Photographs by Harvey Finkle
New York, 1980

POMEGRANATE BOX 6099 ROHNERT PARK CA 94927

Readers

Photographs by Harvey Finkle
New York, 1988

POMEGRANATE BOX 6099 ROHNERT PARK CA 94927

Readers

Photographs by Harvey Finkle
Philadelphia, 1995

POMEGRANATE BOX 6099 ROHNERT PARK CA 94927

Readers

Photographs by Harvey Finkle
New York, 1986

POMEGRANATE BOX 6099 ROHNERT PARK CA 94927

Readers

Photographs by Harvey Finkle

Jerusalem, 1983

POMEGRANATE BOX 6099 ROHNERT PARK CA 94927

Readers

Photographs by Harvey Finkle
Tucson, 1987

POMEGRANATE Box 6099 ROHNERT PARK CA 94927

Readers

Photographs by Harvey Finkle
Philadelphia, 1976

Pomegranate Box 6099 Rohnert Park CA 94927

Readers

Photographs by Harvey Finkle

New York, 1982

Pomegranate Box 6099 Rohnert Park CA 94927

Readers

Photographs by Harvey Finkle

Philadelphia, 1983

Pomegranate Box 6099 Rohnert Park CA 94927

Readers

Photographs by Harvey Finkle

Paris, 1993

POMEGRANATE BOX 6099 ROHNERT PARK CA 94927

Readers

Photographs by Harvey Finkle
Philadelphia, 1979

POMEGRANATE BOX 6099 ROHNERT PARK CA 94927

Readers

Photographs by Harvey Finkle
Tucson, 1987

POMEGRANATE BOX 6099 ROHNERT PARK CA 94927

Readers

Photographs by Harvey Finkle
Philadelphia, 1985

Pomegranate Box 6099 Rohnert Park CA 94927

Readers

Photographs by Harvey Finkle
New York, 1983

POMEGRANATE BOX 6099 ROHNERT PARK CA 94927

Readers

Photographs by Harvey Finkle

Philadelphia, 1984

Pomegranate Box 6099 Rohnert Park CA 94927

Readers

Photographs by Harvey Finkle
Philadelphia, 1983

POMEGRANATE BOX 6099 ROHNERT PARK CA 94927

Readers

Photographs by Harvey Finkle
Paris, 1987

POMEGRANATE BOX 6099 ROHNERT PARK CA 94927

Readers

Photographs by Harvey Finkle
Philadelphia, 1981

POMEGRANATE BOX 6099 ROHNERT PARK CA 94927

Readers

Photographs by Harvey Finkle
Philadelphia, 1982

POMEGRANATE Box 6099 Rohnert Park CA 94927

Readers

Photographs by Harvey Finkle
Philadelphia, 1974

POMEGRANATE BOX 6099 ROHNERT PARK CA 94927

Readers

Photographs by Harvey Finkle
Washington, D.C., 1985

POMEGRANATE BOX 6099 ROHNERT PARK CA 94927

Readers

Photographs by Harvey Finkle
Philadelphia, 1980

POMEGRANATE   BOX 6099   ROHNERT PARK   CA   94927

Readers

Photographs by Harvey Finkle

Philadelphia, 1984

POMEGRANATE BOX 6099 ROHNERT PARK CA 94927

Readers

Photographs by Harvey Finkle
Philadelphia, 1993

POMEGRANATE   BOX 6099   ROHNERT PARK CA 94927

Readers

Photographs by Harvey Finkle
Israel, 1983

POMEGRANATE BOX 6099 ROHNERT PARK CA 94927